Hello, Beautiful!

Zoo Animals

WORLD
BOOK

www.worldbook.com

World Book, Inc.
180 North LaSalle Street, Suite 900
Chicago, Illinois 60601
USA

For information about other World Book
publications, visit our website at
www.worldbook.com or call
1-800-WORLDBK (967-5325).

For information about sales to schools and
libraries, call 1-800-975-3250 (United States),
or 1-800-837-5365 (Canada).

Library of Congress Cataloging-in-Publication
Data for this volume has been applied for.

Hello, Beautiful!
ISBN: 978-0-7166-3567-3 (set, hc.)

Zoo Animals
ISBN: 978-0-7166-3577-2 (hc.)

Also available as:
ISBN: 978-0-7166-3587-1 (e-book)

Printed in China by Shenzhen Wing King Tong
Paper Products Co., Ltd., Shenzhen, Guangdong
1st printing July 2018

Staff

Writer: Grace Guibert

Contents

Introduction

Welcome to "Hello, Beautiful!" picture books!

This book is about animals you might see in a zoo. Each book in the "Hello, Beautiful!" series uses large, colorful photographs and a few words to describe our world to children who are not yet reading on their own or are beginning to learn to read. For the benefit of both grown-up and child readers, a picture key is included in the back of the volume to describe each photograph and specific type of animal in more detail.

"Hello, Beautiful!" books can help pre-readers and starting readers get into the habit of having fun with books and learning from them, too. With pre-readers, a grown-up reader (parent, grandparent, librarian, teacher, older brother or sister) can point to the words on each page as he or she speaks them aloud to help the listening child associate the concept of text with the object or idea it describes.

Large, colorful photographs give pre-readers plenty to see while they listen to the reader. If no reader is available, pre-readers can "read" on their own, turning the pages of the book and speaking their own stories about what they see. For new readers, the photographs provide visual hints about the words on the page. Often, these words describe the specific type of animal shown. This animal may not be representative of all species, or types, of that animal.

This book displays some of the unique animals you may see crawling, climbing, flying, or swinging in a zoo. Zoos often help care for endangered and vulnerable species. Help inspire respect and care for these important and beautiful animals by sharing this "Hello, Beautiful!" book with a child soon.

Hello, beautiful beetle!

You are a green metallic scarab.

You have six legs and two pairs of wings.

Your shiny shell makes you look like a living jewel!

Bird

Hello, beautiful bird!

You are a kookaburra.

You have a long bill.
You use it to catch small
animals to eat.

Your call sounds like
a person laughing!

Chimpanzee

Hello, beautiful chimpanzee!

You are a smart, playful, and curious animal.

You show off your swinging skills on ropes and vines!

Elephant

Hello, beautiful elephant!

You are an African elephant.

You are the biggest animal that lives on land!

You have a long trunk for a nose. You use it like a hand to pick things up!

Fox

Hello, beautiful fox!

You are a fennec.

You are a very small type of fox. But your ears are very big!

You dig a hole to rest in during the day.

Giraffe

Hello, beautiful giraffe!

You are the tallest animal! You have a long neck and four long legs.

You and your giraffe friends each have your own special coat pattern.

Koala

Hello, beautiful koala!

You spend almost all your time in trees.

You look like a teddy bear. But you are not a bear at all!

Orangutan

Hello, beautiful orangutan!

You are a Sumatran orangutan.

You are a red-haired ape.

You like to climb, swing, and play at the zoo. This is what you do in your rain forest home!

Polar bear

Hello, beautiful
polar bear!

You have white fur.
It matches the snowy
places where you live.

Your zoo home has a place
for you to swim. You love
to play in water and on land.

Rhinoceros

Hello, beautiful rhinoceros!

You are a white rhinoceros.

You have big, curved horns on your nose.

You like to stay in the shade to keep cool!

Snake

Hello, beautiful snake!

You are a Burmese python.

You have large **brown** and **black** spots down your back.

You slither around your tank.

You swallow your food whole!

Tiger

Hello, beautiful tiger!

You are a Siberian tiger.

You have an **orange** coat with **black** stripes.

You might be sleeping when we see you in the zoo because you play at night!

Picture Key

Find out more about these zoo animals! Use the picture keys below to learn where each animal comes from, how big it grows, and what each animal eats!

Beetle

Hello, beautiful beetle!

You are a green metallic scarab.

You have six legs and two pairs of wings.

Your shiny shell makes you look like a living jewel!

Pages 6-7 Beetle

Scarabs are a large family of beetles. There are tens of thousands of *species* (kinds). Many are known for their bright, metallic colors. Adults may reach several inches or centimeters in length. Scarabs eat plants, fruit, fungi, *carrion* (dead and decaying animal flesh), and insects.

Bird

Ha ha! Ha ha!

Hello, beautiful bird!

You are a kookaburra.

You have a long bill. You use it to catch small animals to eat.

Your call sounds like a person laughing!

Pages 8-9 Bird

The kookaburra *(KUK uh BUR uh)* lives in Australia and New Guinea. They are about 17 inches (43 centimeters) long. Kookaburras eat caterpillars, fish, frogs, insects, small mammals, snakes, worms, and even small birds.

Chimpanzee

Hello, beautiful chimpanzee!

You are a smart, playful, and curious animal.

You show off your swinging skills on ropes and vines!

Pages 10-11 Chimpanzee

Chimpanzees *(CHIHMP pan ZEEZ or chihm PAN zeez)* live in tropical Africa, from Lake Victoria in the east to the country of Gambia in the west. They range in height from 3 ¼ feet to 5 ½ feet (100 to 170 centimeters) and weigh about 65 to 130 pounds (30 to 60 kilograms). Chimpanzees mainly eat fruits, leaves, nuts, seeds, and stems. They also eat birds' eggs and insects, and sometimes even kill and eat baboons, wild hogs, monkeys, and small antelope.

Elephant

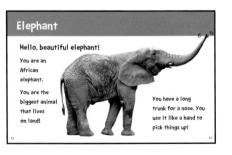

Hello, beautiful elephant!

You are an African elephant.

You are the biggest animal that lives on land.

You have a long trunk for a nose. You use it like a hand to pick things up!

Pages 12-13 Elephant

The African elephant lives only in Africa south of the Sahara. They are the largest type of elephant. (Asian elephants are smaller.) African elephant *bulls* (males) stand about 11 feet (3.4 meters) tall at the shoulder and weigh up to 12,000 pounds (5,400 kilograms). *Cows* (females) are smaller. They are about 9 feet (2.8 meters) tall and weigh about 8,000 pounds (3,600 kilograms). Elephants eat grass, water plants, and the leaves, roots, bark, branches, and fruit of trees and shrubs.

Fox

Hello, beautiful fox!

You are a fennec.

You are a very small type of fox. But your ears are very big!

You dig a hole to rest in during the day.

Pages 14-15 Fox

The fennec *(FEHN ehk)* is the smallest kind of fox. It stands about 8 inches (20 centimeters) tall at the shoulders and weighs about 3 pounds (1.35 kilograms). Its enormous ears grow about 5 inches (13 centimeters) long. Fennecs live in the deserts of northern Africa and the Arabian Peninsula. They hunt locusts, lizards, or small mammals. They also forage for birds' eggs, plant bulbs, and fruits.

Giraffe

Hello, beautiful giraffe!

You are the tallest animal! You have a long neck and four long legs.

You and your giraffe friends each have your own special coat pattern.

Pages 16-17 Giraffe

Giraffes *(juh RAFS)* live in open woodlands, savannas, and deserts in Africa south of the Sahara. Most adult male giraffes stand at just over 17 feet (5.2 meters) tall, and most females grow to about 14 feet (4.3 meters) tall. They feed mostly on the leaves, seeds, twigs, and flowers of trees and bushes.

Koala

Hello, beautiful koala!

You spend almost all your time in trees.

You look like a teddy bear. But you are not a bear at all!

Pages 18-19 Koala

The koala *(koh AH luh)* lives in eucalyptus *(YOO kuh LIHP tuhs)* trees in Australia. Koalas measure from 25 to 30 inches (64 to 76 centimeters) in length and weigh 15 to 30 pounds (7 to 14 kilograms). They eat eucalyptus leaves and shoots.

Orangutan

Hello, beautiful orangutan!

You are a Sumatran orangutan.

You are a red-haired ape.

You like to climb, swing, and play at the zoo. This is what you do in your rain forest home!

Pages 20-21 Orangutan

The Sumatran orangutan *(su MAH truhn oh RANG uh tan)* lives in tropical rain forests on the island of Sumatra in the western part of the country of Indonesia in Southeast Asia. Males grow to about 4 ¹/₂ feet (140 centimeters) tall and weigh about 180 pounds (80 kilograms). Females are about half as large as males. Orangutans prefer to eat ripe fruits, but will also eat leaves, bark, insects, and meat.

Polar bear

Hello, beautiful polar bear!

You have white fur. It matches the snowy places where you live.

Your zoo home has a place for you to swim. You love to play in water and on land.

Pages 22-23 Polar bear

Polar bears live in regions where the sea freezes in winter, mainly along the northern coasts and islands of Alaska, Canada, Greenland, Norway, and Russia. Polar bears range throughout the Arctic Ocean as far north as the North Pole but are more common near land. From nose to tail, adult males measure from 7 ¹/₂ to 8 ¹/₂ feet (2.3 to 2.6 meters) long. Some weigh more than 1,300 pounds (590 kilograms). Females are smaller. Polar bears primarily hunt seals for food.

Rhinoceros

Hello, beautiful rhinoceros!

You are a white rhinoceros.

You have big, curved horns on your nose.

You like to stay in the shade to keep cool!

Pages 24-25 Rhinoceros

The white rhinoceros *(ry NOS uhr uhs)* is native to southern Africa. It is the largest of all rhinoceroses. The white rhinoceros stands about 5 to 6 feet (1.5 to 1.8 meters) tall. Some may grow to over 6 feet (1.8 meters) tall and 15 feet (4.6 meters) long. The white rhinoceros weighs up to 4 tons (3.6 metric tons). Rhinos eat mostly grass.

Snake

Hello, beautiful snake!

You are a Burmese python.

You have large brown and black spots down your back.

You slither around your tank. You swallow your food whole!

Pages 26-27 Snake

The Burmese python *(PY thahn)* lives throughout much of Southeast Asia. They can grow to more than 20 feet (6 meters) long and weigh more than 250 pounds (110 kilograms). Pythons are *constrictors*, meaning that they squeeze their prey to death. Burmese pythons eat small mammals and birds.

Tiger

Hello, beautiful tiger!

You are a Siberian tiger.

You have an orange coat with black stripes.

You might be sleeping when we see you in the zoo because you play at night!

Pages 28-29 Tiger

The Siberian tiger is found mainly in Russia. Adult male tigers reach about 9 feet (2.7 meters) in length, including the tail. They are the world's largest cats. Wild Siberian tigers hunt for such animals as elk, deer, and wild boar.

Index